CAST IN METAL

The Historic Markers

of Oneida County

Copyright © 1998

by

Raymond F. Ball

First Edition

NEW YORK

THE STATE OF LEARNING

THE STATE EDUCATION DEPARTMENT / THE UNIVERSITY OF THE STATE OF NEW YORK / ALBANY, NY 12230

HISTORICAL SURVEY, Room CEC 3097, Empire State Plaza, Albany, NY 12230
Phone: 518 486-2037 Fax: 518 473-8496 E-Mail: plord@mail.nysed.gov Web: http://www.nysm.nysed.gov

March 3, 1998

Mr. Ray Ball
Historical Marker Project
Oneida County Bicentennial Comm.

Dear Ray,

With all the talk these days about "heritage tourism" it may be worth thinking for a moment about New York State's original heritage tourism program – the State Historic Markers. This initiative was begun in 1926 to celebrate the Sesquicentennial of the American Revolution, and undertook to acquaint people newly liberated by the automobile with the history of places they were seeing for the first time.

Of course in those days a drive in the country might involve speeds slow enough to permit the entire text of a marker to be read while passing, and one could stop momentarily if need be without risking life and limb. It is hard to imagine a time when traveling was so slow paced, but it is not at all hard to understand the motivation of people all those decades ago who sought to erect these descriptive captions on the endless exhibit of New York History which every roadside presented to the ever curious "tourist".

Certainly there are few counties as rich in the full breadth of historic sites, and the events they represent, as Oneida County. And in this year of its bicentennial it is notable that its citizens have focused on the remnant historic site markers as a worthy and meaningful project in historic preservation and interpretation. In these times when so many of these old metal signs languish in need of attention, that the residents of Oneida County have undertaken to refurbish those within their borders speaks loudly of the value still placed on these markers, many of which remain the only visible evidence of a past all too often displaced from our landscape and from our memories.

But even more, the effort to make these markers accessible to the modern traveler, the local historian, teachers, students, and local residents alike by publishing a visual guide to these signs truly represents the best in commemorative programming. Everyone connected with this project is to be commended for their spirit and their efforts.

Sincerely,

Philip Lord, Jr.
Acting Chief of the Historical Survey

CAST IN METAL

INTRODUCTION

In 1995 the State Museum in Albany sent a letter to all Towns and Town Historians asking us to complete a survey on our "Historic Markers". This survey asked for information on the content of the marker, where it was located, and the condition of the marker. Apparently the State Museum had thoughts of compiling this information into a report or book.

The concept of this idea stirred our imagination into thinking of what a great thing this would be as an aid in teaching local history in our grade schools. Since we do go into some schools each semester and talk about a local history subject, we were in a good position to discuss the idea with teachers. They were instantly enthusiastic.

Next came the research on each marker. We obtained lists of markers from libraries, historic societies and the county highway department. As we proceeded, other markers were located by word of mouth, rumors and plain good luck. These lists were compared to the survey lists made for the state museum and compiled by the Rome Historic Society.

Then my wife and I began our many field trips to gather information and photograph each marker. This proved to be much fun and we found each trip to be like an exciting mini-vacation. We were like explorers searching for lost treasure.

And search we did — on main roads, but more often on side roads, country dirt roads, farm fields, back yards, cemeteries and private property. People were great. No matter where we went everyone was helpful and friendly. Did we learn? This experience was one of the most educational and interesting events you could ask for. Having lived in Oneida County all our lives we tended to think we knew all about our surroundings, but our numerous trips showed us how much we never knew and had to learn.

We traveled almost nine hundred miles and never left Oneida County. We discovered pleasures — of being on Star Hill on a crisp fall day and seeing Oneida County spread out for miles; of walking along the tow path of the Old Erie Canal; of tracing the steps of the Indian braves as they carried Chief Skenandoah to his final resting place next to his friend Samuel Kirkland at Hamilton College Cemetery; of the 1812 arsenal building; of standing in amazement and pride in front of the historic marker at the B-52 aircraft display.

I remember one day, when giving a talk on local history to a school class, a young boy spoke up and said that his dad told him that their house was built in an old hay field, so what history could there be around here?

We hope this book will answer that question and that all children will come to know there is a lot more than hayfields. We hope parents will become excited and will lay out trips to take their children on in Oneida County to discover and enjoy. We hope young and old will be aroused to go and see what's all around us and "local tourism" will become part of our lives.

Appreciate and enjoy our local history. It's truly wonderful.

Raymond F. Ball
Historian - Town of Marcy

ACKNOWLEDGMENTS

- *To my wife Marion for her patience and help in preparing this book and being my co-pilot on our many research trips.*

- *To town clerks and town historians in every municipality for assistance and guidance.*

- *To Oneida County highway department people for all kinds of assistance.*

- *To many librarians and historic societies for information.*

- *To all the members of the Bi-Centennial Committee for encouragement and help to make this book a reality.*

- *To Muriel D'Agostino and the Daughters of the American Revolution (DAR) for their interest and encouragement.*

- *To everyone we met in our travels for the positive thinking and help to get this work published.*

- *And especially:*

  To Utica Post 229, American Legion for outstanding kindness and assistance. Were it not for Utica Post 229 this book would probably not have been published.

ALPHABETICAL INDEX

There is no numerical index for this book.

Rather, the information is arranged alphabetical by Towns and Cities. The name of each community is given at the top of the pages.

Water Wheel Mill

Band Stand
Taberg

Methodist Church
Taberg

NO KNOWN HISTORIC MARKERS

During the research time in preparing this book every effort was made to locate all historic markers in this town.

If anyone knows of the existence of a marker, either the traditional type or a bronze plaque on stone, please contact the author and we will gladly include it in the next printing.

AUGUSTA

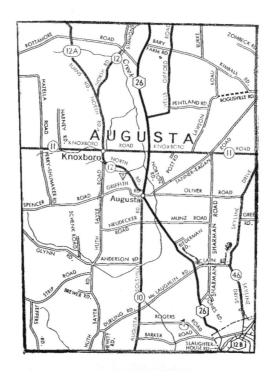

TREATY OF 1760
PROPERTY LINE, INDICATING
FRENCH AND ENGLISH LAND IN
AMERICA, PASSED THIS POINT
WATERSHED FOR ST. LAWRENCE
AND HUDSON RIVERS.

TOWN OF AUGUSTA
1998

There are two of these markers both
identical indicating the property line.

1st -on Rt. 26 at the corner of McLain Road.

2nd - on the Solsville-Augusta Road at the corner of
Durling Road.

← On Rt. 26 across from St. Joseph's church rectory in Oriskany Falls.

← On Rt. 26 - 12B in the center of the Town of Oriskany Falls at the curve in the road.

This is the original church made of local stone.

In Oriskany Falls on Rt. 26 and 12B near the bridge. →

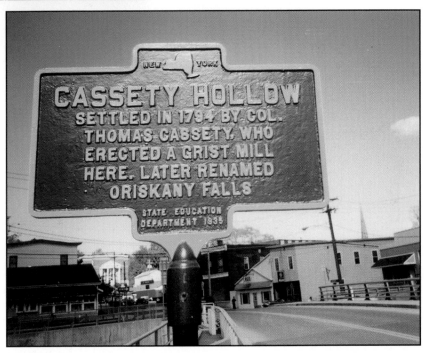

AUGUSTA
ONEIDA COUNTY
MARCH 15, 1798
FORMED FROM THE
TOWN OF WHITESTOWN
TOWN OF AUGUSTA
1998

← On Rt. 26 in Augusta at the entrance to the church parking lot.

Note: There are 3 markers in this church area.

On Rt. 26 across the road from Augusta church (above) parking lot. →

AUGUSTA ACADEMY
FORMED 1834, SEMICIRCULAR
STONE BUILDING USED UNTIL
1878. ITS UNIQUE DESIGN
WAS A CURIOSITY. FIRST
TEACHER, MELVILLE ADAMS
TOWN OF AUGUSTA
1998

AUGUSTA CHURCH
ORGANIZED 1797, BY
CONGREGATIONAL SOCIETY
STATE EDUCATION
DEPARTMENT 1935

← West side of Rt. 26, Augusta Center, in front of the church.

AMOS PARKER
1762 – 1842
TALLEST MAN IN AMERICAN ARMY;
SAVED GEN. LAFAYETTE'S LIFE.
PRESENT AT THE SURRENDER
OF CORNWALLIS. BURIED HERE.
STATE EDUCATION
DEPARTMENT 1935

← At the corner of the Augusta-Solsville Rd., and the Anderson Road.

This man's exact height will probably never be known to us as the army did not keep such good records in the early days. Legend has it that he was almost 8 feet tall.

DR. A. BURGOYNE
1737–1824
BURIED IN THIS CEMETERY. WAS
PHYSICIAN AT SARATOGA UNDER
GEN. BURGOYNE, 1777. LIVED
WITH DAUGHTER IN AUGUSTA.
STATE EDUCATION
DEPARTMENT 1935

← East side of Sayer-Huth Road, at the entrance to Knoxboro Cemetery.

KNOX HOUSE
BUILT 1820 BY
GEN. J. J. KNOX 1791-1876
PIONEER SETTLER,
VILLAGE OF KNOXBORO NAMED
IN HIS HONOR
TOWN OF AUGUSTA
1936

SITE OF
LOG SCHOOL
FIRST IN AUGUSTA BUILT 1797.
AUGUSTA THEN KNOWN AS
BARTLETT'S CORNER USED AS
CHURCH AND MEETING HOUSE
STATE EDUCATION
DEPARTMENT 1935

West side of South Street, Knoxboro, in front of the Knox house.

Formerly located on the northwest corner of Newell's corners. Now on the west side of the Solsville-Augusta Road near stone school house in Augusta.

NEW YORK

SITE OF
LOCK COMPANY
ORGANIZED 1861, BY J. C.
KNOX. HIGH GRADE LOCKS
WERE MANUFACTURED HERE
FOR A NUMBER OF YEARS.
STATE EDUCATION
DEPARTMENT 1935

North side of West St., Knoxboro above the old creamery entrance.

NEW YORK

INDIAN TRAIL
USED BY ONEIDA, TUSCARORA,
BROTHERTON AND STOCKBRIDGE
INDIANS AS A CHANNEL OF
COMMERCE ABOUT 1700. MADE
HIGHWAY SOON AFTER 1800
STATE EDUCATION
DEPARTMENT 1935

North side of West St., Knoxboro, just below the crest off the hill.

NEW YORK

UNION CHURCH
BUILT 1849 BY METHODISTS
AND PRESBYTERIANS. LUMBER
HAULED FROM OLD CHURCH BUILT
ABOUT 1800 ON EAST HILLS.
CONVERTED TO SCHOOL 1873
STATE EDUCATION
DEPARTMENT 1935

East side of South St., Knoxboro in front of the old school.

Located on Broad St. about 1/4 mile from Rts. 12B and 26 in Oriskany Falls.

On the west side of Skyline Drive about 1/2 mile from Oriskany Falls.

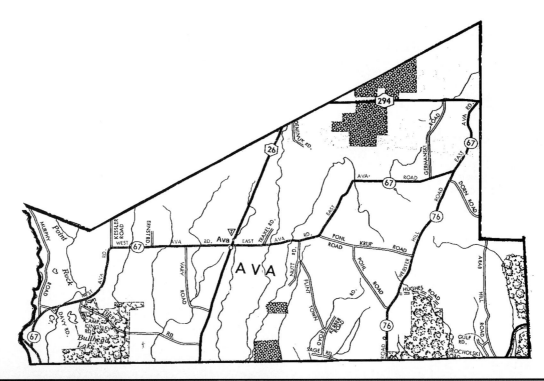

Located on Webster Hill Rd., north side near Sage road.

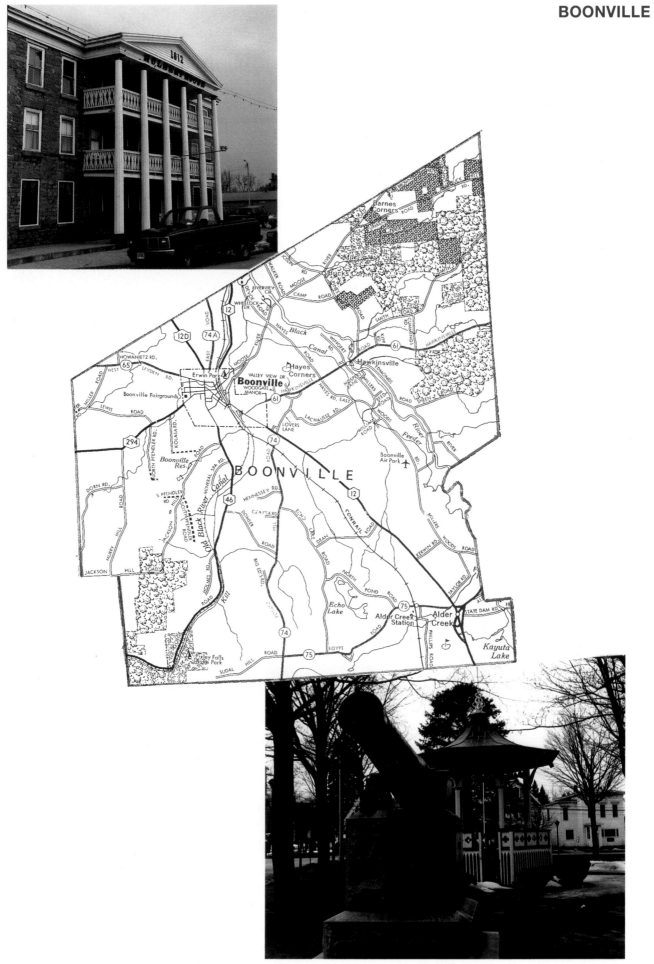

BOONVILLE

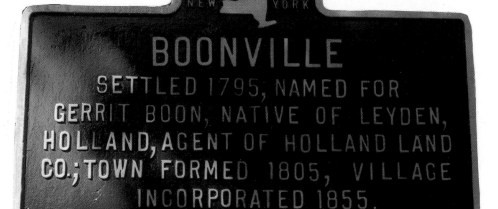

In the town park on Main Street, near the band stand.

BOONVILLE
SETTLED 1795, NAMED FOR GERRIT BOON, NATIVE OF LEYDEN, HOLLAND, AGENT OF HOLLAND LAND CO.; TOWN FORMED 1805, VILLAGE INCORPORATED 1855.

STATE EDUCATION DEPARTMENT 1947

BLACK RIVER CANAL
SITE OF THE ONCE FAMOUS FIVE COMBINES - WORLD'S RECORD FOR NUMBER OF CANAL LOCKS; CANAL HAS 109 LOCKS IN 35 MILES OF WATERWAY

STATE EDUCATION DEPARTMENT 1938

Near Pixley Falls and Holmes Road.

On Rt. 46, two miles north of Pixley Falls (also called the Pixley Falls Gorge Road), the marker is near the edge of the lock.
Use caution.

BLACK RIVER CANAL
1837 - 1922
CONNECTED MOHAWK VALLEY WITH BLACK RIVER COUNTRY OPENING UP 90 MILES OF NAVIGABLE WATERWAY

ONEIDA COUNTY
D.P.W. 1958

On Rt. 12 going into Boonville at the corner of Lovers Lane Road.

OLD FRENCH ROAD
BUILT BY FRENCH COLONISTS, 1790 ON WAY TO SETTLE CATORLAND; FIRST ROAD TO NORTH COUNTRY, FOLLOWING AN IROQUOIS WAR TRAIL.

STATE EDUCATION DEPARTMENT 1936

1859 - 1947

BIRTHPLACE OF APIKUNI
JAMES WILLARD SCHULTZ
BROTHER TO THE BLACKFEET
AUTHOR - EXPLORER - HISTORIAN
FRIENDS OF J.W.S.

At Schuyler Street near Summit St. in the fairgrounds area.

FIRST PRESBYTERIAN CHURCH
SOCIETY ORGANIZED 1805
PRESENT EDIFICE BUILT 1855-56
RE-DEDICATED 1955

STATE EDUCATION DEPARTMENT 1955

Near the corner of James and Church Street in the town.

BOONVILLE

HISTORICAL
MARKER

POST HOUSE, 1817
FIRST USED AS A SCHOOL,
LATER BOUGHT WITH LARGE
TRACT OF LAND BY JOHN G. POST.
PASSED FROM FAMILY IN 1905.

ONEIDA COUNTY
D.P.W. 1969

At the corner of Ford Street and Route 46 (Post Street), by the parking lot at the corner. Marker is near the buildings.

NEW YORK

BLACK RIVER CANAL
SITE OF LOCK 71, SUMMIT
LEVEL; 710 FEET ABOVE ROME;
FROM HERE WATER FLOWED
NORTH TO ST LAWRENCE,
SOUTH TO MOHAWK.

STATE EDUCATION
DEPARTMENT 1938

South side of Schuyler Street and Route 12.

Hop Barn
Route 8

19th Century Book Store
Corner of Rts. 8 and 20

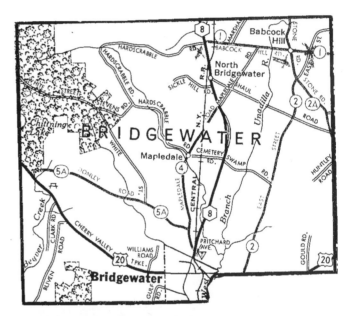

Round Cobblestone Hop Kiln, Roue 8

BRIDGEWATER

← On Rt. 8 outside of Bridgewater, just before Otsego County line.

Masonic Lodge
Route 20

← Babcock Hill Road and East Street.

Steven Moulton Babcock
Originally there were two identical markers, one on each side of Route 8 at Babcock Hill Road.
Both markers are missing?

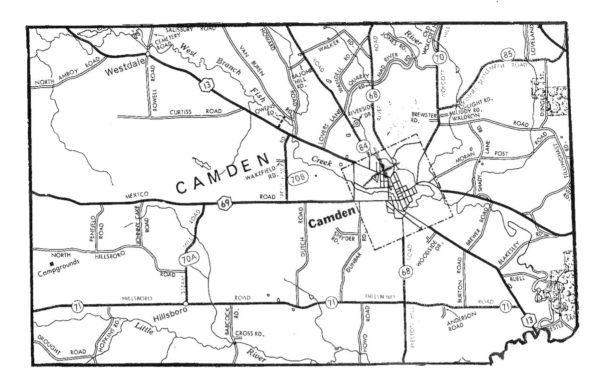

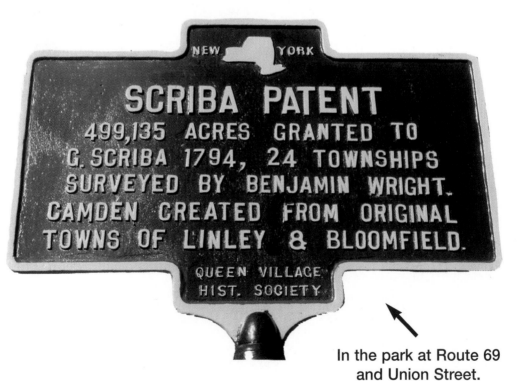

NEW YORK

SCRIBA PATENT
499,135 ACRES GRANTED TO G. SCRIBA 1794, 24 TOWNSHIPS SURVEYED BY BENJAMIN WRIGHT. CAMDEN CREATED FROM ORIGINAL TOWNS OF LINLEY & BLOOMFIELD.

QUEEN VILLAGE
HIST. SOCIETY

In the park at Route 69 and Union Street.

CAMDEN

By the Camden Fire Station located on Rt. 69.

On State Rt. 69 in front of the cemetery.

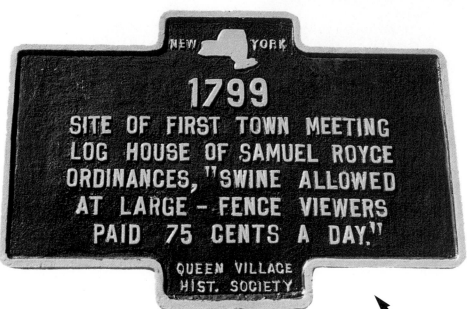

By Camden Elementary School Rt. 13 - River Road.

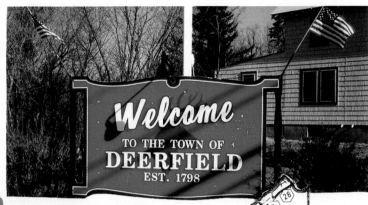

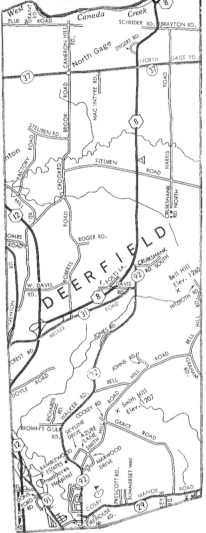

DEERFIELD
ONEIDA COUNTY
MARCH 15TH 1798
FORMED FROM THE
TOWN OF SCHUYLER
HERKIMER COUNTY

STATE EDUCATION
DEPARTMENT 1935

On Old Rt. 8 (Coventry
Ave.) at the corner of
Cosby Manor Rd.
on the north side.

At the corner of Trenton Road
and Fire House Road by the fire
station. This is more a direction
marker to a historic site.

17 MILES
TOMB OF
BARON STEUBEN
IN STATE MEMORIAL PARK
NEAR REMSEN

STATE EDUCATION
DEPARTMENT 1932

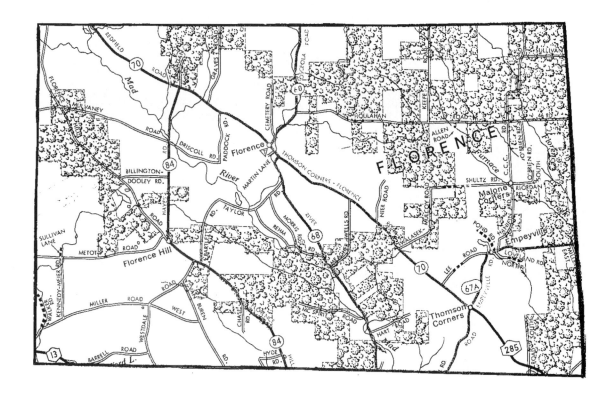

HERE STOOD FOR MORE THAN A CENTURY
THE LAST REMAINING CEDAR MILE POST
MARKING THE ROUTE FROM ROME TO
SACKETTS HARBOR, OVER WHICH
TROOPS MARCHED IN THE WAR OF 1812.

ERECTED BY CAMDEN CHAPTER
DAUGHTERS OF THE AMERICAN REVOLUTION
OCTOBER 31, 1913

⬆ Located on Route 70 (which is the extension of Route
285 out of Taberg) on the left hand side between
Thompson Corners and Florence.

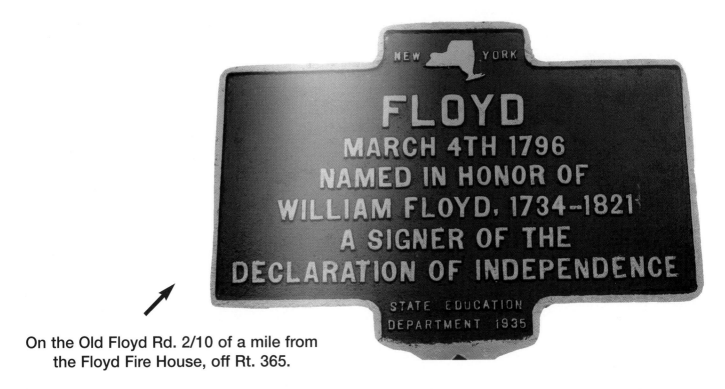

On the Old Floyd Rd. 2/10 of a mile from the Floyd Fire House, off Rt. 365.

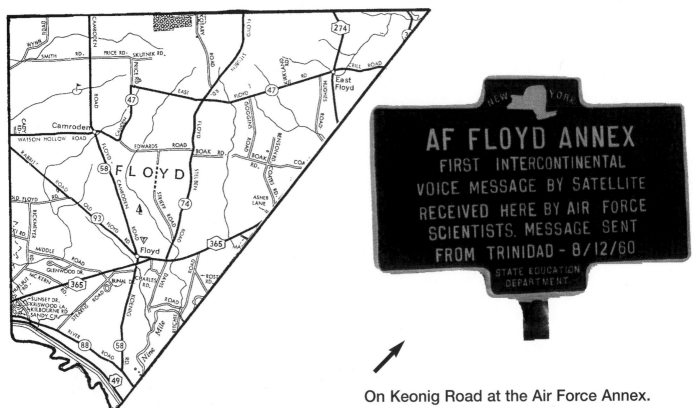

On Keonig Road at the Air Force Annex.

This air force site has been abandoned and mostly torn down. The marker is missing.

A new identical marker is planned, and may be located at the air force laboratory at the former Griffiss Air Force Base in Rome.

FORESTPORT

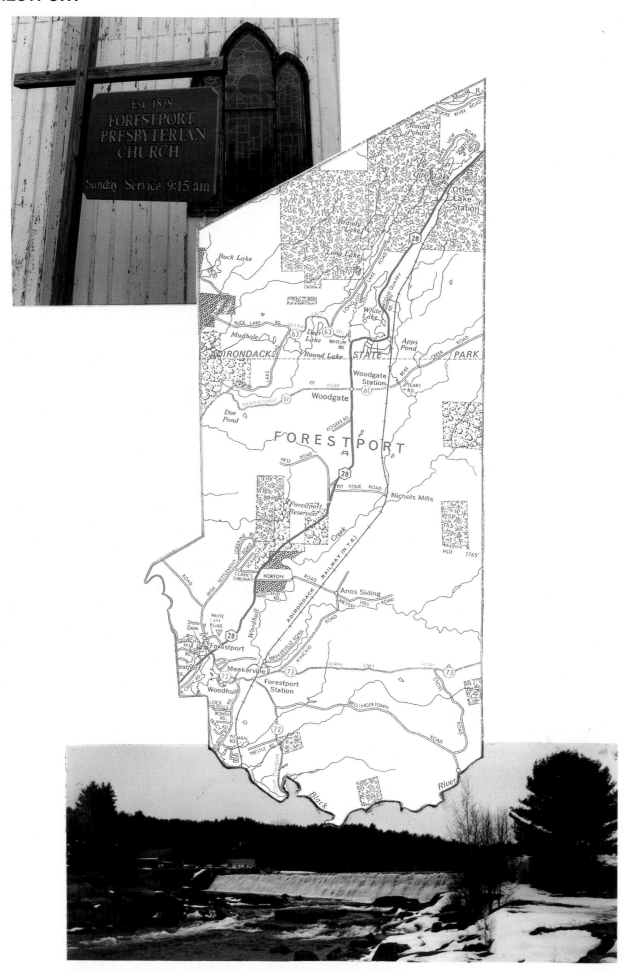

At the corner of River Street and White Lake St. by the church.

N.Y.S. MUSIC CAMP ORIGINAL SITE OF THE OTTER LAKE HOTEL 1893-1946 & NEW YORK STATE MUSIC CAMP 1947-1955. NOW KNOWN AS THE HARTWICK COLLEGE SUMMER MUSIC FESTIVAL & INSTITUTE.

ONEONTA, NY FOUNDER F. SWIFT

Located on Route 28, on the left hand side near the blinking caution lights just before the Fire Dept. building.

North Lake Rd., about 3 miles east of Forestport. The marker is on the right side of the road in a wooded area.

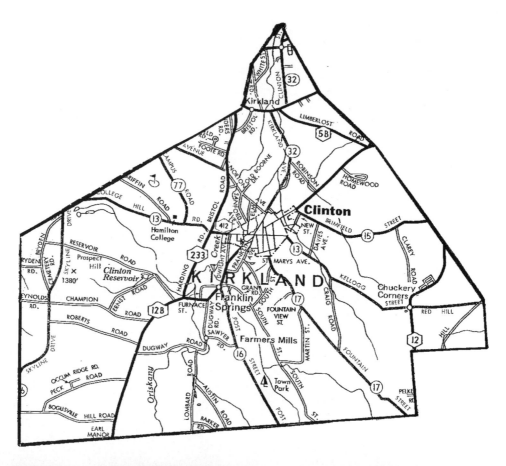

In Clinton on College Street, just west of the intersection of Rt. 12B. →

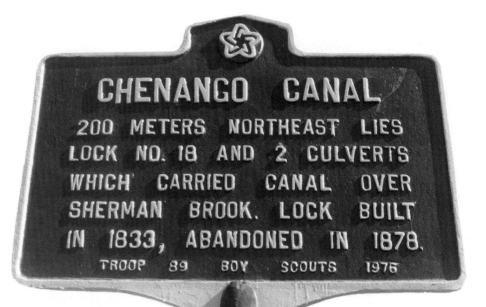

CHENANGO CANAL
200 METERS NORTHEAST LIES
LOCK NO. 18 AND 2 CULVERTS
WHICH CARRIED CANAL OVER
SHERMAN BROOK. LOCK BUILT
IN 1833, ABANDONED IN 1878.
TROOP 89 BOY SCOUTS 1976

HISTORICAL MARKER
SAMSON OCCOM
INDIAN PREACHER OF THE
BROTHERTOWN INDIANS, BELIEVED
TO BE BURIED IN CEMETERY
¼ MILE SOUTH OF HERE.
ONEIDA COUNTY
D.P.W. 1969

← On Boguisville Rd., south of Clinton on Rt. 12B.

On Chestnut Street at the intersection with Williams Street. →

AMERICAN RED CROSS
CLARA BARTON,
FOUNDER OF THE AMERICAN RED
CROSS, ATTENDED THE CLINTON
LIBERAL INSTITUTE, HERE ON
THIS HISTORIC SPOT, WHILE
LIVING IN CLINTON, 1850-1852.

On Hamilton College campus in Clinton. Campus Road in front of the chapel.

On the Hamilton College campus in Clinton. The upper part of Campus Road in front of the small white frame house by the Emerson Art Gallery.

By mailbox 54 on Kirkland Ave., north of Norton Ave.

Burial place of Oneida Chief Skenandoah, who died in 1816 at age 110.
The "White Man's Friend" buried near his friend Samuel Kirkland in the cemetery
at Hamilton College, College Hill Road, Clinton. (See also Vernon).

The original home of Barnabas Pond.

KIRKLAND

At the corner of Rt. 33 and Foote Road, by the pine trees in Clinton.

On College St., Clinton, close to Chenango Ave.

On Kirkland Ave., just north of Chenango Ave., Clinton.

On College St., Clinton, by the creek bridge just east of Rt. 233.

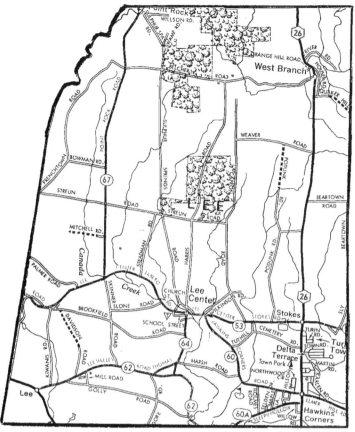

Lake Delta in winter. Under this lake lies the old Village of Delta, which was submerged when Delta Dam was built.

← In front of the house at 6541 Elmer Hill Road within the village.

← History is not all serious long faced people who never smile.

This gentleman realized that his property never has been and probably never will be of historic importance.

His sense of humor is refreshing to all who see his marker. His property didn't make it into our book, but his fun marker did.

On Maynard Drive (old Rt. 49) in front of the Old Maynard School.

MARCY

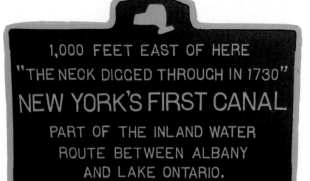

1,000 FEET EAST OF HERE
"THE NECK DIGGED THROUGH IN 1730"
NEW YORK'S FIRST CANAL
PART OF THE INLAND WATER
ROUTE BETWEEN ALBANY
AND LAKE ONTARIO.

← On Mohawk St. between Marcy and Whitesboro, located near the bridge over the Mohawk River.

In front of Whitesboro High School on Rt. 291 in the parking lot in front of the school.

ALUMNI

FIRST
TEACHERS HALL OF FAME
FOUNDED
JULY 7, 1968
BY
WHITESBORO ALUMNI ASSOCIATION
WHITESBORO, N. Y.

GLASSVILLE
IN 1809 THE UTICA GLASS CO.
BEGAN MAKING WINDOW GLASS
HERE. THERE WERE OVER 300
EMPLOYEES, 40 HOUSES AND
2 FACTORY BUILDINGS

On Glass Factory Road about 200 ft. north of Church Rd.

UTICA
MUNICIPAL AIRPORT

SELECTED BY AND SECURED
THROUGH EFFORTS OF AVIATION COMMITTEE
UTICA POST No. 229 AMERICAN LEGION.
PURCHASED AND DEVELOPED DURING
ADMINISTRATION OF
FRED J. RATH
MAYOR

OFFICIAL OPENING JUNE 1st, 1928,
MARKED FIRST LANDING OF
INAUGURAL FLIGHT OF AIRMAIL.

THIS TABLET ERECTED
UNDER AUSPICES OF AVIATION COMMITTEE
UTICA POST No. 229 AMERICAN LEGION
ON OCCASION OF FORMAL DEDICATION
SEPTEMBER 27, 1929.

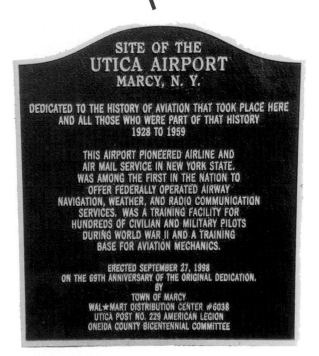

SITE OF THE
UTICA AIRPORT
MARCY, N. Y.

DEDICATED TO THE HISTORY OF AVIATION THAT TOOK PLACE HERE
AND ALL THOSE WHO WERE PART OF THAT HISTORY
1928 TO 1959

THIS AIRPORT PIONEERED AIRLINE AND
AIR MAIL SERVICE IN NEW YORK STATE.
WAS AMONG THE FIRST IN THE NATION TO
OFFER FEDERALLY OPERATED AIRWAY
NAVIGATION, WEATHER, AND RADIO COMMUNICATION
SERVICES. WAS A TRAINING FACILITY FOR
HUNDREDS OF CIVILIAN AND MILITARY PILOTS
DURING WORLD WAR II AND A TRAINING
BASE FOR AVIATION MECHANICS.

ERECTED SEPTEMBER 27, 1998
ON THE 69TH ANNIVERSARY OF THE ORIGINAL DEDICATION,
BY
TOWN OF MARCY
WAL★MART DISTRIBUTION CENTER #6038
UTICA POST NO. 229 AMERICAN LEGION
ONEIDA COUNTY BICENTENNIAL COMMITTEE

AIRPORT MONUMENT

Located on the site of the old Utica Airport, which was on the old River Road west of Marcy State Hospital. This is now the truck entrance to the Wal*Mart Distribution Center.
This plaque on the left is the original, which was on the wall of the hangar which burned down. The one on the right tells about the history of the airport.

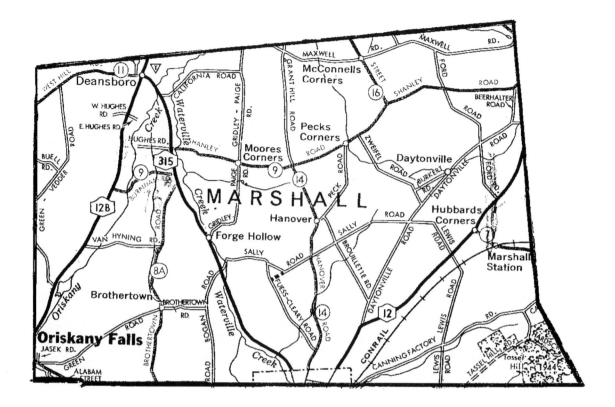

On Rt. 12 at Ford Road north of Hubbards Corners.

The First Forge was erected here in 1801 to manufacture iron from ore. Sherman Daniels and son Charles ran a forge foundry and trip hammer shop here about 1850. They collected large quantities of scrap steel which they reduced into what was known as a loop. These loops were sold to the Remington in Ilion and were used to make gun barrels.

On the left side of Rt. 315 past Gridley-Paige Road at Forge Hollow.

Mounted on a stone monument.

At the corner of Rt. 315 and Burham Road.

BURIAL GROUND OF BROTHERTOWN INDIANS. IN 1783 INDIANS FROM SEVEN NEW ENGLAND TOWNS SETTLED THIS AREA. EMIGRATED TO GREEN BAY, WISCONSIN 1850.

On Rt. 315 in back of Milt Wratten home.

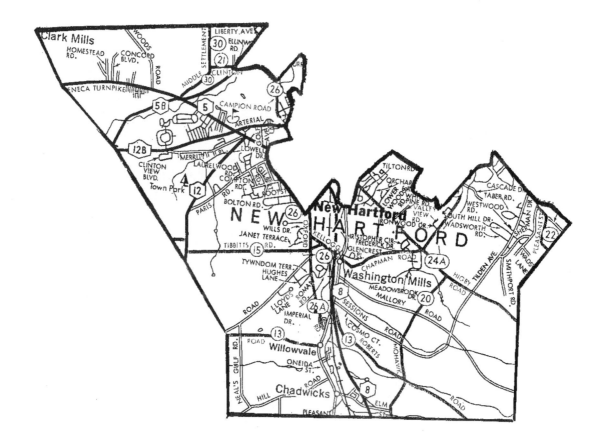

By Pearl and Genesee Streets near the old Point School.

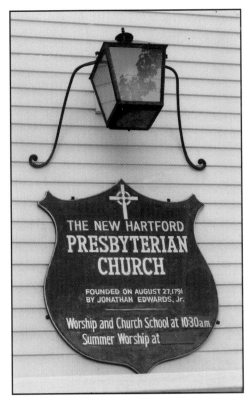

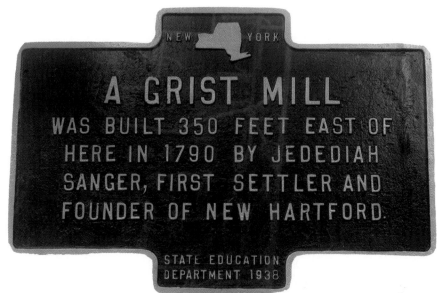

At Oxford Rd and Mill St., across from the fire house.

On the east side of the village park in the center of town. An historic landmark easily seen from all directions by it's majestic steeple.

Rt. 5 near Oxford Road, at Pearl and Genesee St. near the Presbyterian Church.

St. Stephen's Church, Oxford Road.

PARIS

On Rt. 8 at Pinnacle Road in front of the church. →

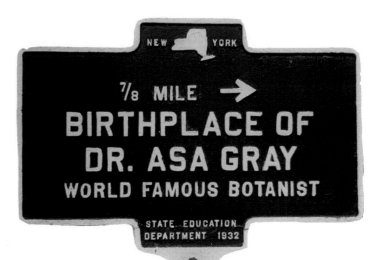

NEW YORK

⅞ MILE →
BIRTHPLACE OF DR. ASA GRAY
WORLD FAMOUS BOTANIST

STATE EDUCATION DEPARTMENT 1932

NEW YORK

FIRST SERMON
PREACHED IN NORTHERN N.Y.
CONFERENCE, 1788, BY ELDER
FREEBORN GARRETSON WITHIN
WHITESTOWN. SAUQUOIT SOC.
FORMED 1788; 1ST IN CONFERENCE.

STATE EDUCATION DEPARTMENT 1939

← At the corner of Mohawk St. and Pinnacle Road on the church's front lawn.

SAINT PAUL'S CHURCH
PARIS HILL, N.Y.
ORGANIZED FEB. 13, 1797

THE OLDEST PARISH IN THE
DIOCESE OF WESTERN NEW YORK
WHEN ORGANIZED NOV. 1, 1838

THIS TABLET COMMEMORATES
THE CENTENNIAL OF THIS DIOCESE
FROM WHICH
THE DIOCESE OF CENTRAL NEW YORK
WAS FORMED IN 1868

THIS TABLET WAS PLACED OCT. 12, 1938

← In the town of Paris along Rt. 12 across from the veteran's monument. The Marker is on a large boulder in front of the church on the village green.

PARIS

The Gray homestead on Pinnacle Road. The house is no longer standing. →

← On Pinnacle Road a few hundred feet east of Mohawk St. on the right side.

A sculpture of Dr. Gray is located in an enclosed court yard off the Botany Dept. at Utica College.

Located on Main Street near the fire house,
(also known as the old Rt. 12) going north.

REMSEN

On Rt. 12 south side just before Fuller Road.

This beautiful sign is not really a marker, but rather a directional sign located on Rt.12, at Star Hill Road in Remsen. It indicates that you turn here to go to the Steuben Memorial.

Note: The Col. Marinus Willett market at Fairchild Road and Rt. 365 is missing. No one seems to know what happened to it:

Col. Marinus Willett
1740-1830
he was second in command
at Fort Stanwix in 1777.

Going north on Main Street in the village make a right turn on to Prospect St. The Chapel is a short distance up the hill on the right side about opposite Lincoln Avenue.

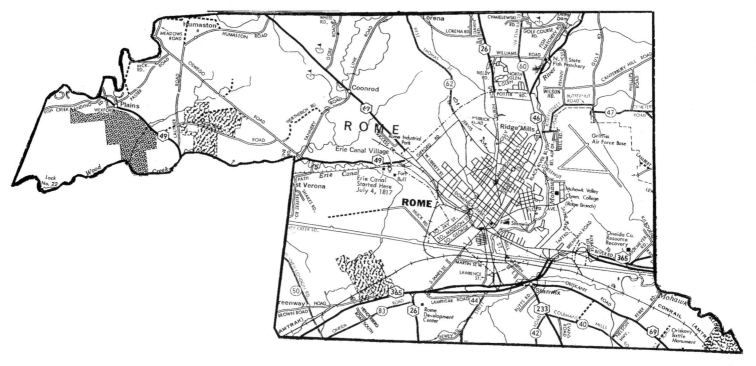

At North James Street in Bellamay Park.

ROME

Route 26 and north Madison St. in the school parking lot.

THE CENTRAL N.Y. SCHOOL FOR THE DEAF FOUNDED JAN. 27, 1875 BY ALPHONSO JOHNSON, THOMAS GALLAUDET AND ROME CITIZENS

STATE EDUCATION DEPARTMENT 1949

ONE BLOCK TO SITE OF FORT NEWPORT AND WOOD CREEK LANDING

N.Y. STATE HISTORICAL MARKER

On the corner of West Dominick and Arsenal Streets.

On West Dominick St. on the north side between Arsenal and Jay Streets.

HISTORICAL MARKER

SITE OF U.S. ARSENAL MAINTAINED AS AN ARSENAL DURING THE WAR OF 1812 AND SUBSEQUENTLY UNTIL 1873.

ONEIDA COUNTY D.P.W. 1970

ROME COURT HOUSE
REBUILT 1849, GREEK REVIVAL STYLE, PUBLIC SQUARE GIVEN BY DOMINICK LYNCH, REPLACED ONE BUILT 1807 AS SYSTEM OF HALF-SHIRE TOWNS BEGAN WINGS AND DOME ADDED 1902

North James St. at Court Street. ←

FIRST CHURCH IN ROME
FIRST PRESBYTERIAN CHURCH
ORGANIZED IN 1800
IN THE HOME OF EBENEZER AND GRACE WRIGHT
AS THE
FIRST RELIGIOUS SOCIETY
OF ROME, N. Y.

PRESENT CHURCH SANCTUARY 1853
SUNDAY SCHOOL ADDITION 1901
CHRISTIAN EDUCATION BUILDING 1959

Located at 108 W. Court Street opposite Bellamy Park. ↑

HISTORICAL MARKER
NORTHWEST 35 RODS
JESSE WILLIAMS
IN 1851 INAUGURATED THE CHEESE FACTORY SYSTEM THUS REVOLUTIONIZING DAIRYING
ONEIDA COUNTY
D.P.W. 1970

Rt. 46 and Fish Hatchery Rd.

HISTORICAL MARKER
THE GRAVE OF
FRANCIS BELLAMY
BORN 1855—DIED 1931
WRITER-EDITOR-PREACHER
IN AUGUST—1892 HE AUTHORED THE PLEDGE OF ALLEGIANCE
ONEIDA COUNTY
D.P.W. 1970

On Jervis Ave at the entrance to the Rome Cemetery. →

ROME

CANAL SITE
OF THE INLAND CANAL BEGUN
IN 1792 AND COMPLETED IN
1797. THE ERIE CANAL WAS
RELOCATED HERE IN 1844

ONEIDA COUNTY
D.P.W. 1970

Erie Blvd. and James
St. on the traffic island.

JOSHUA HATHAWAY HOUSE
BUILT IN 1808 AND MOVED TO
ITS PRESENT SITE IN 1848. IT
WAS JOSHUA HATHAWAY WHO BROKE
GROUND FOR THE ERIE CANAL IN
ROME ON JULY 4, 1817

ONEIDA COUNTY
DPW 1971

Located at 313 North George Street.

THE HOMESTEAD OF
JOHN BLOOMFIELD JERVIS
BORN 1795 – DIED 1885
ENGINEER ON THE ERIE CANAL
CROTON AQUEDUCT FOR N.Y. CITY
FAMOUS HIGHBRIDGE IN HARLEM

ONEIDA COUNTY
D.P.W. 1970

North Washington St., at Elm St. in front of Jervis Library.

Located on James St. on the west side of the fort.
Not a historic marker, but the sign says it all.

On East Bloomfield St. in front of
Staley school., this is mounted on a
boulder next to the historic marker.

ROME

At the intersection of Martin and Mill Streets.

HISTORIC LOWER LANDING PLACE

FOR GENERATIONS, IN SEASONS OF LOW WATER, THE BATEAUX OF TRADERS AND OF THE ARMIES WERE HERE REMOVED FROM THE MOHAWK (AS THE RIVER THEN FLOWED) AND CONVEYED ACROSS THE ONEIDA CARRYING PLACE TO BE RE-LAUNCHED IN WOOD CREEK.

HERE AUG. 2, 1777, LIEUT. HENRY BIRD, COMMANDING ST. LEGER'S ADVANCE GUARD COMPOSED OF 30 REGULARS AND A PARTY OF INDIANS UNDER JOSEPH BRANT, ESTABLISHED THE FIRST CAMP OF THE BRITISH INVESTMENT OF FORT STANWIX. THIS WAS ATTACKED AND LOOTED, AUG. 6, BY LT. COL. MARINUS WILLETT AND 250 CONTINENTAL TROOPS.

CAPT. LERNOULT AND 110 BRITISH REGULARS THEN ERECTED HERE A FORTIFIED CAMP WITH TWO SMALL CANNON AND HELD IT FOR THE REMAINDER OF THE SIEGE.

HERE ALSO WAS THE LOCK, THE STARTING POINT FOR THE FIRST CANAL CONNECTING THE WATERS OF THE MOHAWK AND WOOD CREEK, COMMENCED BY THE WESTERN INLAND LOCK & NAVIGATION CO. IN 1792

NEW YORK STATE HISTORICAL MARKER 1955

Lower landing marker on Martin Street. just west of Mills St., mounted on a large stone located in a small circular park.

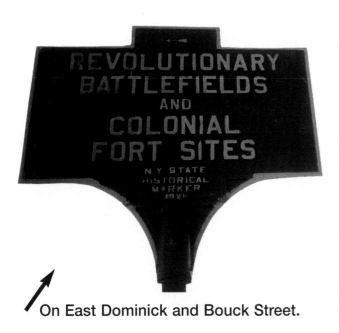

On East Dominick and Bouck Street.

East Bloomfield Street in front of Staley school..

Located at the corner of Liberty and
James Streets.

1755-1756
FORT WILLIAMS
GUARDED
UPPER MOHAWK LANDING
BURNED IN A PANIC
BY BRITISH GEN. WEBB
N Y STATE
HISTORICAL
MARKER
1928

All four of these markers were taken down during the construction of urban renewal projects and/or the reconstruction of Fort Stanwix. They are presently stored in the Rome Historical Society.

FORT BULL
ON WATER ROUTE
DESTROYED AND
MANY KILLED BY
FRENCH & INDIANS
MARCH 27 1756

This marker is carved into the face of a large boulder mounted on a base. It is located on the site of the original Fort Bull on the shore of Wood Creek. The site is at the back of the present Erie Canal Village.

FORT CRAVEN
DESTROYED IN
BRITISH PANIC
BEFORE COMPLETION
AUG. 31 1756

N Y STATE
HISTORICAL
MARKER

NEW YORK

HISTORIC ELM
THIS ELM WAS A SAPLING
GROWING ON THE SOUTHWEST
BASTION OF FORT STANWIX
IN 1804

STATE EDUCATION
DEPARTMENT 1932

HERE THE
ANCIENT CARRY
PASSED SOUTHWARD TO
FORT NEWPORT AND
WOOD CREEK

N Y STATE
HISTORICAL
MARKER
1928

HISTORIC NEW YORK
THE ERIE CANAL · JULY 4, 1817

The ceremonies outside the village of Rome on Independence Day, 1817, climaxed years of discussion about building the Erie Canal. Dignitaries and local citizens assembled at sunrise to attend the start of construction. Judge Joshua Hathaway, a veteran of two American wars, spoke and began the excavation. Judge John Richardson, the first contractor, then turned the earth. Cannon boomed as others started digging.

Benjamin Wright, "the father of American engineering," assisted by John B. Jervis, supervised construction of the section between Utica and the Seneca River. In the first year, 15 miles were constructed. By October, 1819, the 98-mile section was complete, and the first boat traveled from Rome to Utica.

When finished in 1825, the Erie Canal was considered the foremost engineering achievement of the time. The 363-mile Canal crossed the State and became the main route between the Atlantic Ocean and the Great Lakes. Western New York flourished with new, cheap transportation. The canal insured the place of New York City as the nation's greatest port and city, and it hastened development of the Mid-West.

The modernized State Barge Canal System, consisting of the Erie, Champlain, Oswego and Cayuga-Seneca Canals, was completed in 1918.

NEW YORK STATE EDUCATION DEPARTMENT 1907

Bronze marker on posts located just inside Erie Canal Village on Rt. 49 south of Rome.

250 Paces From
Here Is the Site Of
FORT BULL
The Scene Of Fierce
Struggles During The
Early Indian Wars
Twenty Years
Before the Revolution.

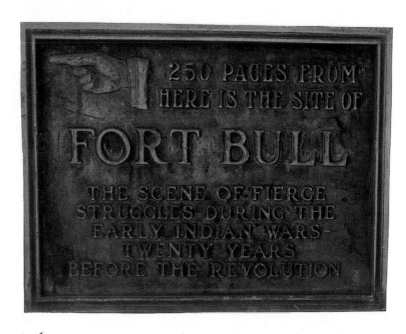

Fort Bull Historic marker at the entrance to the Erie Canal Village.

HISTORICAL MARKER

ERIE CANAL
CONSTRUCTION BEGAN HERE
JULY 4, 1817. FIRST BOAT
TRIP FROM ROME TO UTICA
OCT. 22, 1819. 363 MILE
CANAL COMPLETED OCT. 20, 1825

ONEIDA COUNTY
D.P.W. 1969

On the left side of Rt. 49, south of Rome about 1/2 mile near the Erie Canal Village.

Townscend E. Griffiss
1900 - 1942
Lieutenant Colonel
United States Air Force

———

Lieutenant Colonel Townscend E. Griffiss was born in Buffalo, New York, April 4, 1900 He graduated from the United State Military Academy in 1922 and from Advanced Flying School Kelly Field, Texas in 1924. Colonel Griffiss arrived in the United Kingdom in 1941 and was killed in action when his plane failed to return from a special mission to Moscow, Russia, on February 15, 1942.

Marker is located to the rear of the plane.
→

→
This marker and the missile are located to the left of the B-52 Bomber "The Mohawk Valley", in the picture on the opposite page above right.

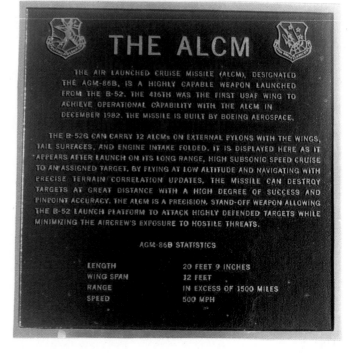

The "Mohawk Valley"
On bronze marker on a large boulder in front of the plane.

An airplane's history is really the story of the men and women who built it, maintained and flew it, as well as the missions it has flown, the places it visited and the accomplishments those people made possible. "225" is here to remember those dedicated people.

The "Mohawk Valley", a G-Model B-523, Tail Number 58-0225, landed at Griffiss for the first time on January 1960, just 7 days after the Boeing Aircraft Corporation finished building it in Wichita, Kansas. Andersen AFB, Guam; Castle AFB, California; and Loring AFB, Maine, were other home bases while the "Mohawk Valley" logged more than 12,000 hours of flight time. Major Bill Penzier, who made 225's first landing at Griffiss in 1960 may not recognize the "BUFF" that Colonel Mike Loughran landed at Griffiss for the last time on 9 May 1991. Throughout its life, extensive modifications, inside and out, kept the airplane an effective weapon system.

The "Mohawk Valley" flew over most of the world's oceans, served with honor in the Vietnam War, trained crews for the Persian Gulf War, and deterred war by standing alert. Then after more than 31 years of service, the "Mohawk Valley" came to this spot, ably assisted by many volunteers, both civilian and military, to stand as a memorial. This airplane represents the men and women of the 416th who "kept'em flying" for over 31 years of continuous B-52G operations.

The name "Mohawk Valley" was on 225 when it first arrived at Griffiss. The mission markings from the Persian Gulf War, symbolize the wing's B-52Gs in that conflict, just prior to converting to the B-52H. The "Ultimate Warrior", tail number 57-6516, was the last B-52G to depart Griffiss, on 8 October 1991. In a sense, the mission markings capture the entire span of the B-52G at Griffiss AFB.

Today, the "Mohawk Valley" stands in tribute to all men and women who dedicate their lives to the defense of our country.

SANGERFIELD

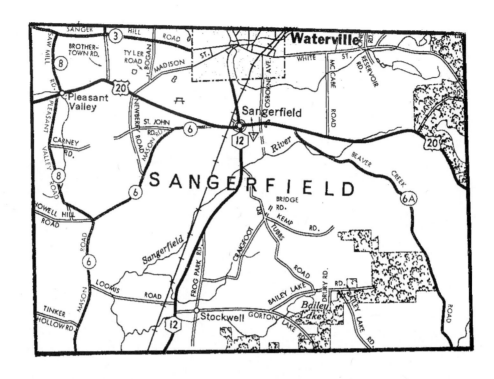

SANGERFIELD
MARCH 5TH 1795
COL. JEDEDIAH SANGER EARLY
SETTLER, BUILT SAW MILL 1793.
WATERVILLE INCORP. FEB 8, 1871
ONEIDA COUNTY
D.P.W. 1968

Located in the Waterville
Village Park

On Stafford Ave. in the
village of Waterville

NEW YORK
SANGERFIELD
ONEIDA COUNTY
MARCH 15TH 1795
TRANSFERRED FROM
CHENANGO COUNTY.
APRIL 4TH 1804
STATE EDUCATION
DEPARTMENT 1935

NEW YORK
BIRTHPLACE OF
GEORGE EASTMAN
INVENTOR OF KODAK
BORN JULY 12, 1854
DIED IN ROCHESTER
MARCH 14, 1932
STATE EDUCATION
DEPARTMENT 1932

Located on Stafford Ave. near the
school house apartment complex in
Waterville.

STEUBEN

Replica of Baron Von Steuben's cabin.

Typical direction markers that can be found in the Town of Steuben and in other towns and cities.

On Star Hill Road, Steuben beyond Fuller Road.

On Fuller Road by house no. 10289, Town of Steuben.

STEUBEN

←

Located on the side of the Methodist Church at the corner of Rt.274 and County Rd. 74 in the Town of Steuben.

On Fuller Road off of Star Hill Road, on the right side in an overgrown field.

→

↗

On Rt. 53 about a half mile from Sixty Road.

In a farm field on Jones Road off Fuller Road. Dirt road going to a farm.

→

Behind the cabin in the park.

←

On Star Hill Road near the back entrance to the park on the left hand side on private property. Located in a cedar hedgerow.

→

On Sixty Road about 1/10th mile south of Star Hill Road.

←

STEUBEN

THIS PARK

WAS CREATED IN MEMORY OF FRIEDRICH WILHELM BARON STEUBEN, MAJOR GENERAL IN THE WAR FOR INDEPENDENCE

STATE EDUCATION DEPARTMENT 1932

On Star Hill Road at Steuben Park, Town of Steuben.

←

In the Steuben Memorial Park.

→

NEW YORK

STEUBEN STATE MEMORIAL PARK

DEDICATED SEPTEMBER 12, 1931 BY FRANKLIN D. ROOSEVELT, GOVERNOR OF NEW YORK

STATE EDUCATION DEPARTMENT 1932

STEUBEN STATE MEMORIAL PARK

INCLUDES FIFTY ACRES GIVEN IN 1804 BY COL. BENJ. WALKER, FRIEND AND AIDE OF STEUBEN TO SECOND BAPTIST CHURCH

STATE EDUCATION DEPARTMENT 1932

At the back entrance to the park by the parking lot.

←

In the park in the scared grove at the grave site.

Monument

STEUBEN

 Mounted on a large boulder near grave site in the sacred grove.

Located in the sacred grove. →

← Located on Fuller Road

A replacement wooden marker made by a very thoughtful person, located on left hand side of Pritchard Rd. 3.5 miles from Rt. 12.

← Actual grave is about 100 feet from the road.

STEUBEN

In a farm field along the power line at Jones Road and Fuller Road. Can not be seen from the road. Requires quite a walk from the road.

In front of cemetery going up Star Hill Road off of Rt.12.

On top of Star Hill on right hand side just above the observation parking area, and just below the radar dome field office.

TRENTON

TRENTON
ONEIDA COUNTY
MARCH 24, 1797
FORMED FROM THE
TOWN OF SCHUYLER,
HERKIMER COUNTY

STATE EDUCATION
DEPARTMENT 1936

On Mappa Ave. almost by
Mill Street in Barneveld.

← Mounted on the front wall of the east church facing the park in Holland Patent.

On Park Ave. next to the Cincinnati Creek on the south side of Barneveld.

Mounted on a large boulder adjacent to the United Methodist Church, on the right hand side.

Fountain Elms on Genesee Street (marker in storage).

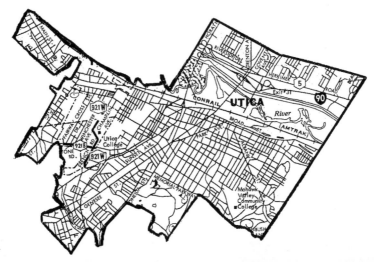

St. Elizabeth's Medical Center, Genesee St. Originally on Columbia Street, where it was founded in 1866 by the Sisters of St. Francis and has been operated by them ever since.

On Charlotte St. on the lawn between the County Court House and the County Office Building.

in the park next to the Children's Museum on Main St., Utica, west of the railroad station.

On Sherman Drive in front of the college library.

On Oneida Street at the entrance to Forest Hill Cemetery.

ROUTE OF THE NEW YORK,
WEST SHORE
& BUFFALO RR, BUILT 1881-84
TO RIVAL NY CENTRAL. LEASED
BY NYC 1885. PENN-CENTRAL
FORMED 1968. ABANDONED 1971
U&MV CHAPTER, NRHS 1995

On Holland Ave., the left side just off the Parkway.

←

This marker is located on the lawn in front of the Utica Public Library on Genesee Street.

→

UTICA PUBLIC LIBRARY
BUILT 1904 - CHARTERED 1893
HAS BEEN LISTED ON THE
STATE AND NATIONAL
REGISTERS OF HISTORIC
PLACES - OCTOBER 29, 1982.

On Herkimer Road., North Utica. A short distance past the intersection with Avert Ave. Many years ago this area was part of the Town of Deerfield.

→

FIRST BAPTIST
CHURCH OF NORTH UTICA
FOUNDED 1798 - BUILT 1811
LISTED STATE AND NATIONAL
REGISTERS OF HISTORIC
PLACES JULY 11, 1985

This marker is mounted on the wall at the Hanna Park at the corner of Genesee and Columbia Streets.

This bronze marker is attached to the east end of the warehouse building located on Broad St at the corner of Mohawk. The marker is facing north.

Located on the upper road going around a corner of the property line of Forest Hill Cemetery, Oneida St.

His grave is located in Lot No. 38 in Forest Hill Cemetery not far from the historic marker.

Note: Cemetery regulations do not allow historic markers within the cemetery. Therefore you will generally find markers along the road close to the grave within the cemetery.

THE HISTORICAL AND PATRIOTIC SOCIETIES OF UTICA PLACE THIS STONE TO MARK THE SITE OF ONE OF A CHAIN OF FORTS BUILT TO PROTECT THE NORTHERN FRONTIER FROM THE FRENCH AND THEIR INDIAN ALLIES, AND TO GUARD THE GREAT FORD ACROSS THE MOHAWK RIVER.

ONEIDA HISTORICAL SOCIETY,
DAUGHTERS OF THE AMERICAN REVOLUTION,   UTICA
SONS OF THE REVOLUTION,   OCT. 12, 1910.
CHILDREN OF THE AMERICAN REVOLUTION,

On a boulder in Baggs Hotel Park, Main Street, just west of the Railroad Station near the Children's Museum.

· ON THIS SITE ·
THE HOLY SACRIFICE OF THE MASS
WAS FIRST OFFERED IN UTICA, IN 1813.
· BY THE ·
REV. PAUL McQUADE
A MISSIONARY FROM ALBANY

ERECTED BY
SANTE FE CARAVAN, No. 40
ORDER OF ALGAMBRA
UTICA, N.Y. —— 1922

On the corner of Broad St. and Second St. This was the home of the Devereux family who were prominent merchants and started the Savings Bank of Utica. The home is now gone.

THE GRAVE OF
GOVERNOR HORATIO SEYMOUR
BORN 1810 — DIED 1886
GOVERNOR OF NEW YORK
1853 TO 1855 AND 1863 TO 1865
PRESIDENTIAL CANDIDATE IN 1868

On the east side of Oneida St. between Ferris and Geer Ave. outside Forest Hill Cemetery. Located on top of a concrete retaining wall.

UTICA

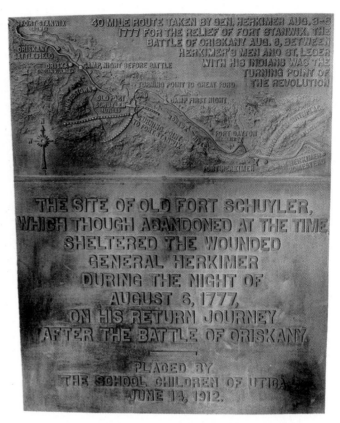

Both of the above markers are in Baggs Square Park on Main Street west of the railroad station.

Located on French Road, Utica, where the road goes under Route 12 (north/south arterial). It's on the right hand side of French Road heading south toward New Hartford.

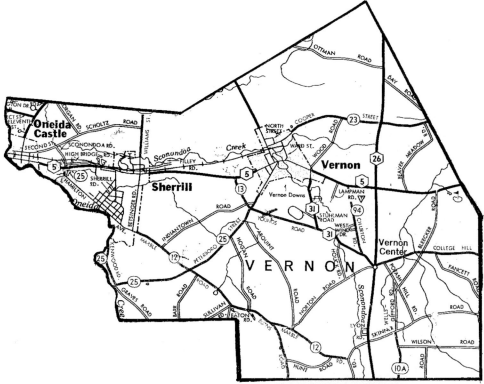

Tilden Hill Farm is a 150 acre farm that has been in the Brewer family for seven generations. Founded in 1798 by Josiah Brewer, the farm has served as a grist mill, chicken farm, cheese factory, and a fruit and vegetable farm.

VERNON

VERNON BANK
FOUNDED AND BUILT IN 1839
BY ABRAHAM VAN EPS AND
JOHN KNOX. CHARTERED AS A
NATIONAL BANK IN 1865
VERNON
HISTORICAL SOC.

On Route 5 (Seneca Street) in front of the bank, on the left side facing west, opposite the fire house.

Located on Route 5 (Seneca St.) next to the fire hall, on the right hand side facing west.

NEW YORK

MISSION CHURCH
OF ONEIDA INDIANS, BUILT 1818
AT ONEIDA CASTLE BY REV. ELEAZAR
WILLIAMS. MOVED HERE IN 1842
BY UNITARIANS. BECAME VERNON
TOWN HALL 1892.

STATE EDUCATION
DEPARTMENT 1949

PETTIBONE FARM
BUILT ABOUT 1799 BY
ABIJAH BRONSON, AN EARLY
VERNON SETTLER. PURCHASED
BY STATE SENATOR
JARED C. PETTIBONE IN 1842
VERNON
HISTORICAL SOC.

On Youngs Road between Peterboro Street and Rt. 31.

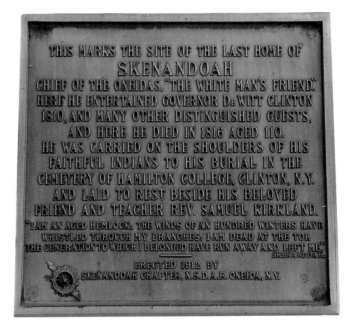

Located on Rt. 5 in Oneida Castle. The original lettering was ruined by salt and it is now painted as shown. This is a marker next to the actual boulder.

Bronze marker mounted on a large boulder. In Oneida Castle on Rt.5 at the corner of High Bridge Road, opposite West Hamilton Rd. The boulder is on the right side going west.

Also see Town of Kirkland for the Hamilton College Cemetery for the burial place of Chief Skenandoah.

Located on Marble Hill Road about 1/8 mile west of Peterboro Street.

VERNONA

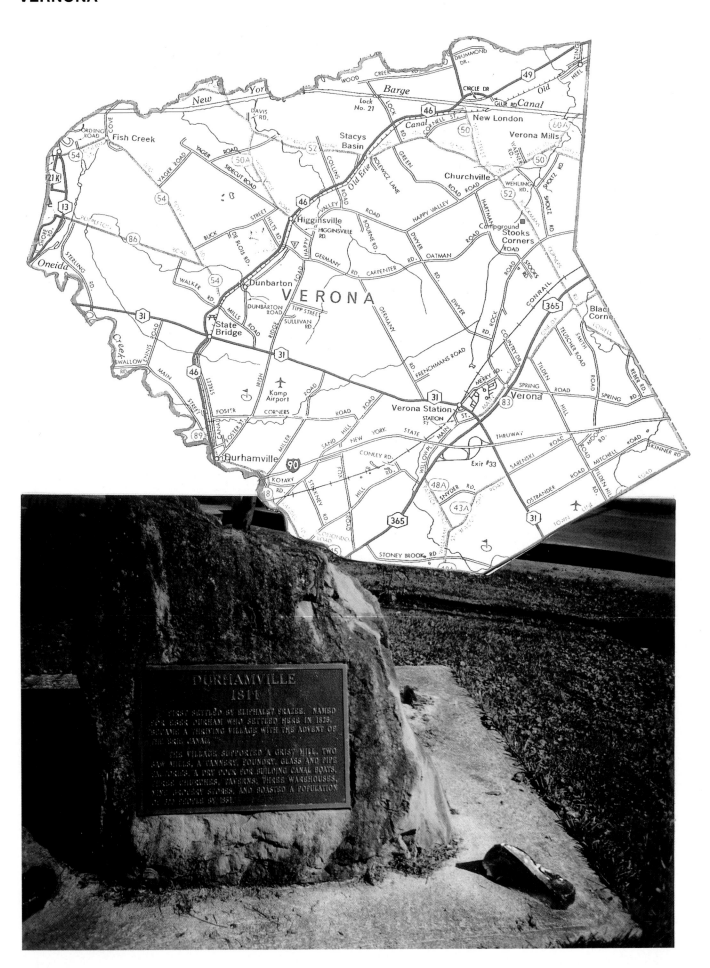

DURHAMVILLE
1811

FIRST SETTLED BY ELIPHALET FRAZEE. NAMED
FOR EBER DURHAM WHO SETTLED HERE IN 1826.
BECAME A THRIVING VILLAGE WITH THE ADVENT OF
THE ERIE CANAL.

THE VILLAGE SUPPORTED A GRIST MILL, TWO
SAW MILLS, A TANNERY, FOUNDRY, GLASS AND PIPE
FACTORIES, A DRY DOCK FOR BUILDING CANAL BOATS,
THREE CHURCHES, TAVERNS, THREE WAREHOUSES,
NINE GROCERY STORES, AND BOASTED A POPULATION
OF 600 PEOPLE BY 1851.

Bronze marker on a large boulder just off Rt. 46 at
the intersection of Canal and Broad Streets (small
park) There are chunks of glass from the old glass
factory around the base of the boulder.

HISTORIC NEW YORK

THE ERIE CANAL - THE LONG LEVEL

Construction of the Erie Canal began at Rome on July 4, 1817, to take
advantage of the "long level." That portion of the canal between Utica and
Salina (now Syracuse) was planned first because there were relatively few
obstructions and because the level surface required no locks. In October,
1819, the 98-mile section between Utica and the Seneca River was completed,
and the first boat traveled from Rome to Utica.

The State-financed Erie Canal was constructed by local contractors
who used their ingenuity to build a canal across New York, then largely a
wilderness. The 363-mile canal was 40 feet wide and four feet deep; 83 locks
took it over different land levels. The canal was hailed as the foremost
engineering achievement of the time.

When finished in 1825, the Erie Canal became the main route between
the Atlantic Ocean and the Great Lakes. Western New York flourished with
cheap, new transportation. The canal insured the place of New York City as the
nation's greatest port and city, and it hastened development of the Mid-West.

The modernized State Barge Canal System, consisting of the Erie,
Champlain, Oswego and Cayuga-Seneca Canals, was completed in 1918.

EDUCATION DEPARTMENT   STATE OF NEW YORK 1967   DEPARTMENT OF PUBLIC WORKS

On Route 46 about half a mile north of Rt. 31 on the bank of the
Erie Canal. Located in a State Parking area opposite Walker Road.
Some thoughtless people have put graffiti on this marker.

VERONA

On Germany Rd at the corner of Rt. 46 and Higginsville.

Located on the left side of Rt. 13 at the beginning of the bridge going over the canal towards Sylvan Beach. Also known as Canal Street and Lake Shore Road.

On New London Road about 100 feet off Rt.46 by the old canal.

VIENNA

HISTORICAL MARKER

GRAVE OF CAPT. ADJ.

GEORGE MARSDEN

STAFF OFFICER OF

GEN. GEORGE WASHINGTON

SEE PLAQUE AT GRAVE

ONEIDA COUNTY
D.P.W.   1968

Located in the Village of Jewell on Rt. 49 in front of a small cemetery.

THE GRAVES OF
CAPTAIN AND ADJUTANT
GEORGE MARSDEN,
PERSONAL FRIEND AND
STAFF OFFICER OF
GENERAL GEORGE WASHINGTON,
WHO DIED NOV. 12, 1817,
AGED 80 YEARS.

ALSO HIS WIFE
WILMUTH LEE, OF VIRGINIA,
SISTER OF RICHARD HENRY LEE,
A SIGNER OF THE
DECLARATION OF INDEPENDENCE,
WHO DIED JAN'Y 13, 1850,
AGED 93 YEARS.

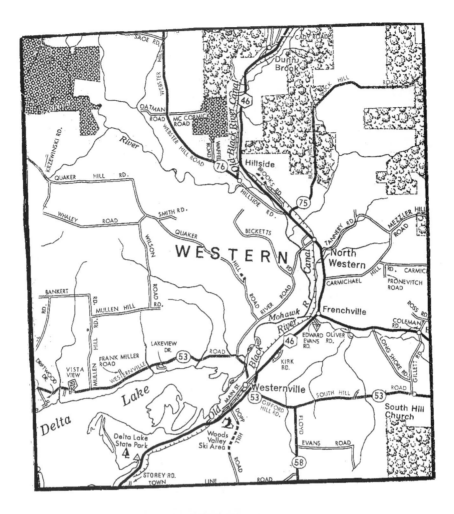

On Main Street in Westernville in front of the library.

HISTORICAL
MARKER

THE HOMESTEAD OF
GENERAL WILLIAM FLOYD
BORN 1734 – DIED 1821
MEMBER OF THE CONTINENTAL
CONGRESS. SIGNER OF THE
DECLARATION OF INDEPENDENCE

ONEIDA COUNTY
D.P.W. 1970

On Main Street in Westernville.

1734   1821

THIS MARKS THE HOME OF
GENERAL WILLIAM FLOYD,
A SIGNER OF
THE DECLARATION OF INDEPENDENCE,
REPRESENTATIVE IN CONGRESS
AND NEW YORK STATE SENATE,
BURIED IN WESTERNVILLE CEMETERY.

ERECTED BY
GENERAL WILLIAM FLOYD CHAPTER
DAUGHTERS OF THE AMERICAN REVOLUTION
OF BOONVILLE, NEW YORK.

Marker on the boulder in front of
General Floyd's homestead.

NEW YORK

11 MILES
TOMB OF
BARON STEUBEN
IN STATE MEMORIAL PARK
NEAR REMSEN

STATE EDUCATION
DEPARTMENT 1932

At the corner of Rt. 46 and
Rt. 274.

Located on the Stokes Western Rd about a tenth of a mile from Main Street, on the right hand side in front of the church.

The grave is located in the cemetery, which is right behind the church.

In Memory of
General William Floyd
Who died August 4, 1821 aged 87 years.
He was born at Mastic on Long Island.
An ardent supporter of his country's rights.
He was honored in life for the sincerity of his
Patriotism and the Declaration of Independence
Will be to his memory an imperishable monument.

WESTMORELAND

On Rt. 26 at the bridge going over the
Thruway. Use caution as no stopping or
parking is allowed on the bridge.

Located in a row of bushes by a house numbered 7366, on
Stone Road near the new Town Hall driveway. Rather difficult
to see.

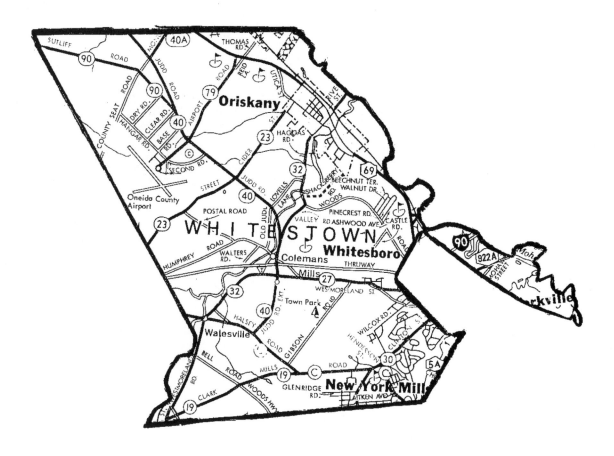

On Main Street in the Village of Whitesboro in front
of Dunham Library.

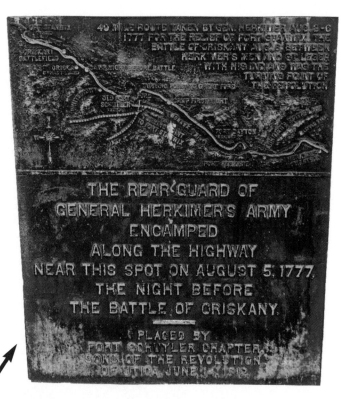

At the corner of Main Street and Tracey Ave. in Whitesboro. The original church has been replaced with a modern structure.

A bronze marker on a large stone in front of Dunham Library, Main St., Whitesboro.

This is one of 14 such markers between Little Falls and Rome. They were erected by the Daughters of the American Revolution to honor General Herkimer's Army.

Located in front of the Town Hall on Park Ave. facing the village park.

On Whitesboro Street in the Village of Yorkville, just past the intersection with Rt. 5. On the north side of the the road, the house itself recently burned down.

NEW YORK
ENGLISH HOME
BUILT 1792. BIRTH PLACE OF
HENRY INMAN, 1801-46
ARTIST WHO EXCELLED IN
PORTRAITS, LANDSCAPES
AND MINIATURES
STATE EDUCATION
DEPARTMENT 1932

NEW YORK
IST PRESBYTERIAN CHURCH
OF WHITESBORO
ORGANIZED APRIL 1, 1793
BETHUEL DODD, IST PASTOR
STATE EDUCATION
DEPARTMENT 1932

On Main Street in the Village of Whitesboro near Elm St.

On Rt. 69 near River Street in the Village of Oriskany, on the south side of the road.

HISTORICAL MARKER
SITE OF
WOOLEN MILL
ERECTED IN 1810
BELIEVED TO BE THE 1ST.
IN AMERICA TO MANUFACTURE
FABRICS FROM RAW MATERIAL
ONEIDA COUNTY
D.P.W. 1968

NEW YORK

HERE STOOD THE HOME OF
COLONEL GERRIT
G. LANSING
OFFICER IN CONT. ARMY
WHO PURCHASED LAND WHEREON
ORISKANY WAS FOUNDED 1802

STATE EDUCATION
DEPARTMENT 1932

Located at Dexter St. and Utica St. in the Village of Oriskany.

Bronze marker on a boulder at the same location as the above marker.

HERE AT THE ENTRANCE OF THE GROUNDS
OF COL. GERRIT G. LANSING
STOOD THE TWO OAKS UNDERNEATH WHICH
THE MARQUIS DE LA FAYETTE
COL. LANSING'S COMPANION IN ARMS
AT YORKTOWN
WAS RECEIVED ON THE MORNING
OF JUNE 10, 1825
BY THE RESIDENTS OF ORISKANY

MARKER PLACED BY
THE ORISKANY CHAPTER
DAUGHTERS OF THE AMERICAN REVOLUTION
JUNE 1923

Oriskany Monument

The Oriskany Monument was dedicated on August 6, 1884, 107 years after the Battle of Oriskany. During it's 150th anniversary in 1927, five acres of the battlefield, including the monument, were made a New York State historic site to serve as a memorial to those who fought so bravely and tenaciously to preserve their land and freedom. Additional acreage has been acquired through the years, and in 1963 the United States Department of the Interior, in recognition of the site's exceptional value in commemorating and illustrating the history of the United States, designated Oriskany Battlefield a National Historic Landmark.

THE MILITARY ROAD

Joseph Brant, familiar with the terrain, probably selected the place of ambush - where a small stream crossed the military road. The military road of 1777 was about ten rods north of the present highway.

Both these markers are located within the Oriskany Battlefield Park.

AMBUSH STARTED HERE

The militia column, on its way to the relief of Fort Stanwix, marched into this ravine, August 6, 1777, and were ambushed by Loyalists and British. The attackers came out of hiding in woods on the west, the south and the north.

THE RALLY

Both sides regrouped during a driving rain. Herkimer's troops concentrated here, forming an irregular circle. The attackers were on all sides.

"In the Valley homes was great mourning. For such a small population, the losses were almost overwhelming. In some families the male members were wiped out. It was many a long, weary year before the sorrow and suffering caused by the sacrifices at Oriskany had been forgotton in the Valley of the Mohawk."

Nelson Greene, *History of the Mohawk Valley*

These posts Erected by the Oriskany Chapter Daughters of the American Revolution Organized with the Special object of making a National Park of the Oriskany Battlefield 1929.

Many families lost more than one of their family at Oriskany. Perhaps the greatest lost was to the Snell family, who lost seven out of nine who fought there.

← Near this spot
Stood the beech tree
Which during the Battle of Oriskany
sheltered the wounded Gen. Herkimer
while he gave orders
that made Saratoga possible
and decided the fate of the Nation.

ORISKANY BATTLEFIELD

The Battle of Oriskany, fought on August 6, 1777 has been described as one of the bloodiest battles of the American Revolution. This fight for freedom, however was not in vain since it was a significant factor in the turning point of the war. The war, thus far, had brought a series of disasters to the armies of the rebellious colonies. It was the intention of the British to split the colonies by gaining control of New York State, thus dividing the northern states from those in the south. To accomplish this a three-pronged invasion, known as the Campaign of 1777, was planned. General Barry St. Leger, leading an expedition from Oswego, was to go down the Mohawk Valley to Albany. There he would united with the main British forced led by Major General John Burgoyne, coming south from Canada along Lake Champlain and the Hudson River. A third force led by General Sir William Howe, was to advance north from New York City.

St. Leger met unexpected resistance at Fort Stanwix, at that time under the command of Col. Peter Gansevoort. His men laid siege to the fort, which did not fall as easily as St. Leger had anticipated. Up on hearing of the British advance, Brigadier General Nicholas Herkimer assembled 800 Tryon County militia to aid Gansevoort and on August 4 began the forty mile march west from Fort Dayton to Fort Stanwix.

Tory leaders Sir John Johnson and Col. John Butler were sent by St. Leger to ambush Herkimer and his troops. Indians led by Mohawk chief Joseph Brant accompanied the loyalist supporters. They chose a boggy ravine two miles east of the Oriskany Creek as their point of ambush. Unsuspecting, Herkimer's inexperienced militiamen marched blindly into he trap. As they crossed the swampy bottom and marched up the ravine side, the enemy closed in. Muskets blazed from behind trees. Indian tomahawks flashed.

In the first murderous volley, General Herkimer's horse was shot from beneath him and his leg shattered by a musket ball. Sitting beneath a beech tree, propped against his saddle and smoking an old black pipe, Herkimer continued to direct the battle. The patriots fought bravely in hand-to-hand combat, in spite of heavy losses. Their stubborn resistance dismayed Johnson's troops. But the battle was so brutal that many Indians abandoned the fight, forcing the British and Tories to withdraw as well.

The battered patriots returned to their valley homes. Herkimer was taken by raft down the Mohawk River to his home in Little Falls where several days later, after an unskillful amputation of his leg, he died.

The retreating British returned to Stanwix and found that their nearby camp had been raided and valuable supplies captured. The assault against Fort Stanwix continued indecisively. Disgusted, the Indian allies withdrew, forcing St. Leger to abandon the siege and return to Canada.

To the Unknown
Patriotic Soldiers of Tyron County

Who under the leadership of
Colonel Ebenezer Cox   Colonel Jacob Klock
Colonel Peter Bellinger   Colonel Frederick Visscher

followed
HERKIMER
Through the bloody battle of Oriskany, and were here on August 6, 1777
Checked St. Legers advance upon Albany, administering the first defeat to the
Advancing columns of Burgoyne. Their patriotic sacrifices are commemorated
here by the Mohawk Valley Historic Association in the erection of this monu-
ment.

August 6, 1928

The U.S.S. Oriskany, an air craft carrier was named in honor of the Battle of Oriskany. This park is located on the grounds of the Oriskany Museum on Rt. 69 in the Village of Oriskany. The ship's bell, anchor, and fighter plane are from the de-commissioned U.S.S. Oriskany. Bronze markers on stones are located in the park (shown above).

ANCHOR
USS ORISKANY CVA-34

IN MEMORY OF THOSE
WHO SERVED OUR NATION IN
KOREA – VIETNAM
AS DID THE AIRCRAFT CARRIER